WAR GAME

Michael Foreman

This edition first published in Great Britain in 2014 by
Pavilion Children's Books
A division of Anova Books Ltd
10 Southcombe Street, London, W14 0RA

A CIP catalogue record for this book is available from the British Library.

ISBN 978-1-84365-178-9

10 9 8 7 6 5 4 3 2 1

Printed and bound by Toppan Leefung Printing Limited, China

This book can be ordered direct from the publishers at the website
www.anovabooks.com, or try your local bookshop.

The Publishers would like to thank the following for permission to reproduce
illustrative material: Bowman Gray Collection, University of North Carolina
at Chapel Hill pp. 2, 8, 12, 26 and 36; Hulton Picture Library p. 7; Imperial War
Museum pp. 9 and 79 (top left); British Library Newspaper pp. 10 (bottom) and 57;
Tonie & Valmai Holt pp. 10 (top) and 46; Mansell Collection p. 12; John Frost
Historical Newspaper Collection pp. 12 and 57; National Army Museum pp. 76
(bottom right) and 78 (top); Phil Vasili, courtesy of the Finlayson Family p. 79
(Walter Tull photographs). Special thanks also go to Peter Daniels from the
Westminster Archives for his assistance with the text and remaining illustrations
on pp. 76, 77, 78 and 79.

WAR GAME

THE LEGENDARY STORY OF THE
FIRST WORLD WAR FOOTBALL MATCH

Michael Foreman

PAVILION
CHILDREN'S

IN MEMORY OF MY UNCLES, WHO DIED IN THE GREAT WAR.

WILLIAM JAMES FOREMAN, KILLED AGED 18
FREDERICK BENJAMIN FOREMAN, KILLED AGED 20
WILLIAM HENRY GODDARD, KILLED AGED 20
LACY CHRISTMAS GODDARD, DIED OF WOUNDS CHRISTMAS DAY 1918 AGED 24

FOUR AMID A MULTITUDE

Two brothers walked out of my Grandfather's Suffolk cottage amongst the hollyhocks and went to war. Their names are on the village war memorial. A third brother, my father, was too young to go with them.

Two other young men, my mother's brothers, left Granny's Norfolk village pub and went to war. Their names are on another war memorial. There are no photographs of these young men. They didn't live long enough to have children. They left just four names amid a multitude.

My father died one month before I was born … but, back then, all my friends were growing up without their fathers. They were all away in the Second World War. The only local men around were too old for this new war, but were still haunted by the ghosts of the First World War. Soon, however, our village became full of men. Fathers and brothers from other lands, all on their way to war. They trained on our cliffs and beaches, camped in our woods and fields. They made a fuss of us – the last children they would see before hitting the beaches of occupied Europe. And so another multitude went off to war.

As I write this, sitting in our London garden, there are hollyhocks standing to attention in the shade like the hollyhocks around Grandfather's cottage.

There are four of them.

MICHAEL FOREMAN, 2014

THE KICK-OFF

GOAL! Will saw the ball hit the back of the net. In his imagination he had just scored for England, and he heard the roar of a huge crowd. But he knew that around the pitch there was no crowd, just a low hedge and the familiar flat fields of the Suffolk countryside.

A group of small boys jumped around behind the goal and a few old men sitting under the elms clapped. The church clock struck five. The game was over.

The two teams changed and joked together. 'We'll come back and beat you after the war,' laughed one of the opposing team as they began their walk back to their village five miles away.

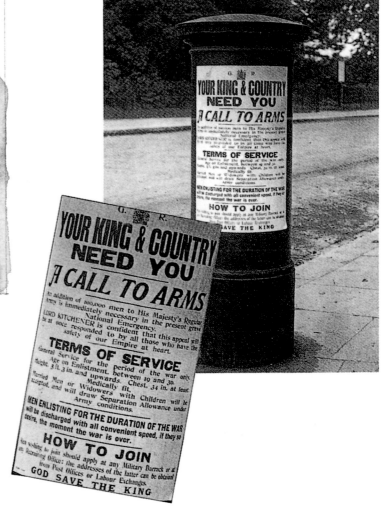

'Most of them are joining the army,' said Freddie, the goalkeeper. 'We should, really.'

'I'd like to,' said Billy, eyes shining with excitement.

'No, you're too young. If you went, I'd have to go to look after you,' laughed his big brother Lacey.

'It *would* be an adventure, though,' said Will.

'And they say it'll be over by Christmas. Be a pity to miss it.'

And so they talked as they wandered back along the dusty lane into the village.

The summer of 1914 had been one of the hottest ever, and while Will and his friends had worked long and hard in the harvest fields, far away in a place called Sarajevo an Archduke had been killed. The German emperor, Kaiser Bill, was using the confusion as an excuse to start a war and seize territory from his neighbouring countries.

'So once again the British Army has to go overseas and sort things out,' said the old men of the village over their pints of beer.

Many of the old soldiers of the village had already been recalled to the army and were on their way to the battlefields of France and Belgium. There was a lot of pressure on the young men to follow them. The British Army needed many thousands of men to stop the Germans advancing across Europe. Recruitment posters were everywhere, and the newspapers called on every man to do his duty 'for King and Country'.

The day after the football match was a Sunday, and the vicar boomed out the same message from his pulpit. The local squire, in the front pew, wore all the medals he could get his hands on, and his son wore a brand-new, tailor-made officer's uniform. After the service, Will, Freddie, Billy and Lacey sat by the signpost under the oak and elm at the corner of the green. Here they had sat almost every day of their lives, after church, after school and after work.

'I think we should join,' said Freddie. 'None of us has ever been outside the county. It's time we saw something of the world.'

'Yes! An adventure – and home by Christmas,' said Billy.

Will wasn't so sure. After all, he thought, a lot of people can get killed in a war. But they agreed that next day after work, they would go into town and see what was happening at the Town Hall, the local army recruiting office.

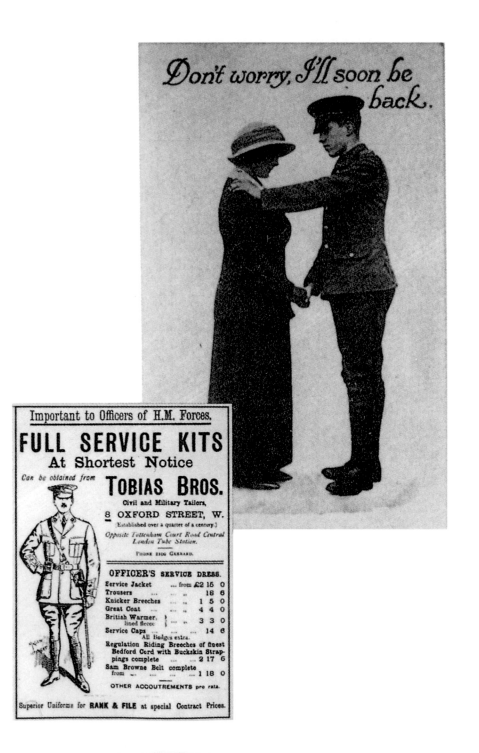

THE ADVENTURE

They had never seen such a crowd. There was a great feeling of excitement and even of fun as the flags waved and the band played. Every time a lad went to join up, the crowd gave him a hearty cheer.

Before anyone could stop him, Billy was up the steps and the crowd was cheering him. Then Freddie followed. Lacey had to go to look after Billy. Will knew he couldn't let his friends go off to war without him, so to wild cheers all four joined the army. They were given railway warrants and told to report to barracks in four days' time.

They had a lot of explaining to do when they got home that evening.

Being country boys, they were all good shots, and they were signed into the Kings Royal Rifles. It sounded very grand. But so great was the rush to join that the army was overwhelmed with recruits and didn't have enough uniforms for them all. Will and the other lads were disappointed and felt foolish learning the basic training and drills wearing their ordinary clothes. They slept in bell tents in a huge field, about a dozen men to a tent. The food was poor and the days were long and exhausting.

However, after a few weeks they were all kitted out and the 'adventure' had really started. They boarded a P&O ship in Southampton and prepared to set sail at six o'clock in a great convoy.

The whole of Southampton turned out to see them off. Thousands of sailors cheered and waved their caps from destroyers in Southampton Water.

As the coast of England faded behind them, Will, like the countless young men crowded around him, felt strangely alone with his thoughts of home and of what lay over the horizon.

'Come on, lads. Let's have a song,' called Freddie. They sang as they sailed and felt better.

TO THE FRONT

When they reached France they were packed into trains, which stopped and started and crawled all day along the overcrowded tracks.

The country didn't look so different. People worked the fields just as the lads had done back home. Some of the workers unbent their backs and waved as the trains went by.

The soldiers finally arrived at a small station that had grown into a
vast supply depot. Trains and trucks were being shunted and unloaded.
Mountains of stores, horse lines and mule lines were everywhere, and
there was a babel of shouted commands.

Then at last they were off the trains and marching. Will felt good to be out in the fresh air and swinging along with his mates. Marching through villages and towns, the troops were cheered all the way. Flowers, fruit and bread were pressed into their arms. It seemed like a pretty good war so far, even though it had begun to rain and the long dry summer was over.

Then things began to change. The roads became crowded with people moving back from the Front. The whole population seemed to be on the move. Families carried their children and pushed prams loaded with whatever they could salvage from their lives. No more cheering crowds. These people had seen war. Their homes had been blown to bits, their farms criss-crossed by armies, trenches, wire and pock-marked by a million artillery shells. Will could hear the almost continuous sound of shellfire in the distance.

They passed wagons full of wounded soldiers on their way back to England, and long lines of exhausted ragged troops sitting in the mud, rain and gathering darkness before being ordered back into the action.

At last the marching came to an end, and Will, Freddie, Lacey and Billy and the rest of the brigade were ordered on to a fleet of London General omnibuses that were to rush them up to the Front to fill a gap in the 'Line'. They drove through the ruins of a devastated town. The lads had never been to London, yet here they were riding on a London bus in the middle of France. The conductor's bell was still working, and one of the men kept ringing it and shouting 'Next stop Piccadilly Circus!' The glassless windows were covered with boards, but there were plenty of holes to peep through. Will's first reaction was: 'Doesn't it look pretty? Just like fireworks.'

Then they were in the trenches. Not the front trench, but the reserve. In single file they moved forward along a winding communication trench to the support trench. Here they waited with the sound of battle exploding all around them.

There was a lull.

'All right, lads. It's our turn,' said their sergeant, and in single file and pouring rain they squelched along another communication trench to the Front.

The trenches of the Western Front crossed Belgium and France for a distance of 460 miles. The Front trench was about three feet wide at the bottom and seven feet high. To enable the soldiers to fire over or through the parapet, a fire-step was built two feet high into the forward side of the trench. It was on this that the sentries stood to keep watch.

Lavatories, or latrines, were dug at the end of short trenches, mostly to the rear of the main trench. Occasionally they were dug a little way forward into No Man's Land to discourage anyone from lingering too long.

There was still no shooting on this section of the Line as Will and his mates crouched on the fire-step to allow wounded and exhausted soldiers to pass by on their way to the rear.

Dogs were sometimes used as sentries in some sections, particularly by the French. Some dogs also searched for wounded men and others were messenger dogs.

NO MAN'S LAND

Will and Freddie were the first to be posted as sentries on their little section, and, cautiously, they stood up on the fire-step. They peered over the parapet into No Man's Land. They could just see their own first line of wire and random humps and bumps in an otherwise flat landscape that seeped rapidly into darkness. A landscape as flat as the fields of home.

Then a flare arced and spiralled slowly from the sky. Will and Freddie could see that the humps and bumps were men. Dead men. Some of them, who had cut their trousers into shorts during the hot weather, looked like fallen schoolboys.

Before the flare faded, Will and Freddie saw more lines of wire and, beyond No Man's Land, the front line of German trenches.

'Less than a goal kick away,' whispered Freddie.

The newcomers quickly learned the routine of trench life. An hour before dawn every morning they received the order to 'Stand To'. Half asleep and frozen, the men climbed on to the fire-step, rifles clutched with numb fingers and bayonets fixed.

The half light of dawn and at dusk was when an attack was most expected, and both sides had their trenches fully manned at those times. Sometimes nothing happened. Often there was a furious exchange of rifle and machine-gun fire to discourage any attack through the gloom. This was known as 'morning hate'.

After an hour or so the order was given to 'Stand Down'. Only the sentries remained on the fire-step and the rest of the men enjoyed what breakfast they could get among the rats, blood-red slugs and horned beetles that infested the trenches.

Each company going to the Front Line took food for three days, usually bully beef, tins of jam and bone-hard biscuit. Army biscuit had to be smashed with a shovel or bayonet. The pieces were then soaked in water for a couple of days and were sometimes added to soup.

Dugouts were dug into the sides of trenches and roofed with timber or corrugated iron and covered with a minimum of 9 inches of earth and sandbags.

Sometimes the rats would suddenly disappear. Old soldiers thought this to be a sure sign of imminent heavy shelling.

As the weather grew worse, the two huge armies became bogged down in virtually fixed positions. In some places they were only thirty yards apart, so close that the heavy guns, firing from behind the reserve lines, often killed their own men when shells fell short of their target.

The mud became deeper and deeper as thousands of men, mules, horses and heavy wagons and guns churned it up.

Now and then the soldiers were ordered to attack across No Man's Land, even though many lives were always lost and little or nothing was achieved. Small raiding parties ventured out at night to cause as much damage as they could, and, if possible, to return with a prisoner or two who could provide some useful information. Other small teams were sent to repair or lay new wire. The covering darkness could be suddenly illuminated at any time by flares. A pistol flare remained bright for about fifteen seconds. This seemed an eternity to men lying motionless in No Man's Land awaiting the rattle of machine-gun fire or a sniper's bullet.

The Germans sometimes used a flare suspended from a small parachute. This blazed brightly for up to a minute, and might be followed by a second and a third flare.

"TUBS FOR TOMMIES".

£10 WILL PROVIDE A UNIT OF 4 BATHS, WITH STOVE, BOILER, TOWELS, SOAP, SCRUBBERS AND ALL EQUIPMENT.

FROM THE EMERGENCY VOLUNTARY AID COMMITTEE OF THE EMPRESS CLUB DOVER STREET W.

SOAP

APPLY TO THE SECRETARY, BRANCH OFFICE 36, QUEEN VICTORIA ST. E.C.

Steel helmets were devised in 1915. In short supply, they were passed from one man to another as the soldiers left the firing line. The Battle of the Somme in 1916 was the first time that all the British soldiers had their own helmets.

The communication trenches were particularly busy at night. Dead and wounded were carried to the rear, and food and munitions were brought to the Front. When possible the dead were recovered from No Man's Land. Like clearing the table after dinner, ready for the Generals' next game of soldiers, Will thought.

Will often thought of his family sleeping peacefully just 100 miles away, and of his own bed, dry and warm under the thatched eaves of home. Even his old dog guarding the yard and the pigs in the byre lived in more comfort than Will and the British Army.

And still it rained.

The water table of this flat land was often less than three feet below the surface. Every shell hole filled with water. The trenches were awash with mud. Here and there men hollowed out little caves or 'scrapes' in the sides of the trenches to give them some protection from the rain, but they had little protection from the high-explosive shells, which could rain down at any moment.

The enemy trenches were so close that whenever the fighting died down, each army could hear the other's voices and could sometimes even smell their breakfast. They all knew that they were sharing the same terrible conditions.

Singing in the trenches was common in 1914, and songs from one front line floated to the other on the quiet evening air. Occasionally during a quiet period a British Tommie would put a tin can on a stick and hold it above the parapet to give the Germans some shooting practice. The Germans would do likewise with tin cans or bottles, and a shooting match would develop accompanied by cheers and boos.

Sometimes the soldiers watched rival aircraft confront each other in mid-air duels over the trenches.

Will, Freddie, Lacey and Billy stayed together as much as possible and lived like bedraggled moles in a world of mud, attack and counter-attack.

The weather, still wet, grew steadily colder.

Then, one night, as the lads returned to the Front after a few days' rest, the rain stopped and it grew bitterly cold.

That night they were relieving a Scottish regiment, and as the Scots left the Line, the Germans shouted Christmas wishes to them.

The primitive warplanes of 1914 were not armed at first and flew on spy missions, spotting enemy gun positions, supply depots and troop movements.

Pilot and observer were usually armed with revolver and rifle respectively. Some carried grenades, which they tried to drop on the trenches.

Then the tiny lights appeared in the German trenches. As far as the eye could see, Christmas trees were flickering along the parapet of the German lines.

It was Christmas Eve.

A single German voice began to sing 'Silent Night'. It was joined by many others.

The British replied with 'The First Noel' to applause from the Germans. And so it went on, turn and turn about. Then both front lines sang 'O Come All Ye Faithful'.

It was a beautiful moonlit night. Occasionally a star shell hung like a Star of Bethlehem.

At dawn, when the British were all 'Stood To' on the fire-step, they saw a world white with frost. The few shattered trees that remained were white. Lines of wire glinted like tinsel. The humps of dead in No Man's Land were like toppled snowmen.

After the singing of the night, the Christmas dawn was strangely quiet. The clock of death had stopped ticking.

Then a German climbed from his trench and planted a Christmas tree in No Man's Land. Freddie, being a goalkeeper and therefore a bit daft, walked out and shook hands with him. Both sides applauded.

A small group of men from each side, unarmed, joined them. They all shook hands. One of the Germans spoke good English and said he hoped the war would end soon because he wanted to return to his job as a taxi driver in Birmingham.

It was agreed that they should take the opportunity to bury the dead. The bodies were mixed up together.
They were sorted out, and a joint burial service was held on the 'halfway line'.

Both sides then returned to their trenches for breakfast. Will and the lads were cheered by the wonderful smell of bacon, and they had a hot breakfast for a change.

One by one, birds began to arrive from all sides. The soldiers hardly ever saw a bird normally, but Will counted at least fifty sparrows hopping around their trench.

Christmas presents for the men consisted of a packet of chocolate, Oxo cubes, a khaki handkerchief, peppermints, camp cocoa, writing paper and a pencil. After breakfast a pair of horses and a wagon arrived with Princess Mary's Christmas gifts – a pipe and tobacco and a Christmas card from the King and Queen.

With our best wishes for Christmas 1914
May God protect you and bring you home safe

Mary R   George R.I.

There were no planes overhead, no observation balloons, no bombs, no rifle fire, no snipers, just an occasional skylark. The early mist lifted to reveal a clear blue sky. The Germans were strolling about on their parapet once more, and waved to the British to join them. Soon there was quite a crowd in No Man's Land. Both sides exchanged small gifts. One German had been a barber in Holborn in London. A chair was placed on the 'halfway line', and he gave haircuts to several of the British soldiers.

Then, from somewhere, a football bounced across the frozen mud. Will was on it in a flash. He trapped the ball with his left foot, flipped it up with his right, and headed it towards Freddie.

Freddie made a spectacular dive, caught the ball in both hands and threw it to a group of Germans.

Immediately a vast, fast and furious football match was underway. Goals were marked by caps. Freddie, of course, was in one goal and a huge German in the other.

Apart from that, it was wonderfully disorganized, part football, part ice-skating, with unknown members on each team. No referee, no account of the score.

It was just terrific to be no longer an army of moles, but up and running on top of the ground that had threatened to entomb them for so long. And this time Will really could hear a big crowd – and he *was* playing for England!

He was playing in his usual centre forward position with Lacey
to his left and little Billy on the wing. The game surged back
and forth across No Man's Land. The goalposts grew larger
as greatcoats and tunics were discarded as the players
warmed to the sport. Khaki and grey mixed together.
Steam rose from their backs, and their faces were
wreathed in smiles and clouds of breath in the
clear frosty air.

Some of the British officers took a dim view of such sport, and when the game to its exhausted end, the men were encouraged back to their trenches for a carol service and supper. The haunting sound of men singing drifted back and forth across No Man's Land in the still night air.

'Good night, Tommies. See you tomorrow.'

'Good night, Fritz. We'll have another game.'

But Boxing Day passed without a game. The officers were alarmed at what had happened on Christmas Day. If such friendly relations continued, how could they get the men to fight again? How could the war continue?

The men were not allowed to leave the trenches.

There were a few secret meetings here and there along the Front, and gifts and souvenirs were exchanged.

It was the Duke of Wellington who gave the nickname 'Tommie' to the British soldiers. When asked in 1843 to think of a name typical of the private soldier, the great duke thought back over his long career to his first campaign in the Low Countries. He remembered a group of wounded men lying on the ground. One of them had a sabre slash in his head, a bayonet wound in his chest, and a bullet through his lungs. He begged not to be moved, but to be left to die in peace. He must have seen Wellington's concern. 'It's all right, sir', he gasped. 'It's all in the day's work.'
'What's your name, soldier?' the Duke asked.
'Thomas Atkins, sir.'
They were his last words.

Two more days passed peacefully. Then a message was thrown over from the German side. A very important general was due to visit their section at 3.15 that afternoon and he would want to see some action. The Germans therefore would start firing at 3pm and the Tommies should please keep their heads down.

At three o'clock a few warning shots were fired over the British trenches and then heavy fire lasted for an hour. The Tommies kept their heads down.

At dawn a few days later, the Germans mounted a full-scale attack. The friendly Germans from Saxony had been withdrawn and replaced by fresh troops from Prussia. They were met by rapid and deadly fire from the British and were forced back.

The order was given to counter-attack, to try to take the German trenches before they could reorganize themselves. Will and the rest of the British soldiers scrambled over the parapet.

Freddie still had the football! He drop-kicked it far into the mist of No Man's Land.
'That'll give someone a surprise,' he said.
'Why are goalies always daft?' thought Will.

They were on the attack. Running in a line, Will in a centre
forward position, Lacey to his left, young Billy on the wing.

From the corner of his eye Will saw Freddie dive
full-length, then curl up as if clutching a ball in the best
goalkeeping tradition.

'Daft as a brush,' Will thought.

Suddenly they all seemed to be tackled at once. The whole
line went down. Earth and sky turned over, and Will found
himself in a shell hole staring at the sky. Then everything
went black.

Slowly the blackness cleared and Will could see the hazy sky once more. Bits of him felt hot and other bits felt very cold. He couldn't move his legs. He heard a slight movement. There was someone else in the shell hole.

Will dimly recognized the gleam of a fixed bayonet and the outline of a German.

'*Wasser. Wasser*,' the German said.

It was about the only German word Will knew. He fumbled for his water bottle and managed to push it towards the German with the butt of his rifle.

The German drank deeply. He didn't have the strength to return the bottle.

'*Kinder?*' he said. Will shook his head. The German held up three fingers. Will tried to shake his head again to show that he did not understand, but the blackness returned.

Later he saw a pale ball of gold in the misty sky. 'There's a ball in
Heaven,' he thought. 'Thank God. We'll all have a game when this
nightmare's over.'

At home when he had a bad dream he knew that if he opened his
eyes, the bad dream would end. But here, his eyes were already open.

Perhaps if he closed them, the nightmare would end.

He closed his eyes.

28 June
Assassination of Archduke
Franz Ferdinand of Austria.

4 August
The five Great Powers are
at war: Russia, France and
Britain against Germany
and Austria-Hungary.

11 August
A Call to Arms!
Lord Kitchener sets out to raise a
new volunteer army of 100,000 men.
Newspapers and posters called on
every man to do his duty 'for King
and Country'.

Pal's Battalions
It was thought that men would be
more willing to join up if they could
serve with people they already
knew. The first 'Pals Battalion' was
formed in Liverpool. Other towns
and cities soon followed. Just like
Will and his pals – brothers, cousins,
friends, workmates and teammates all
enlisted together spurred on by
a spirit of patriotism and promises
of adventure.

22 November
Trenches are formed along the
entire Western Front. Reality
of life in the trenches was far
from the glorious adventure
that the enthusiastic young
recruits had expected.

THE CONTENTS
OF THE PRINCESS
MARY GIFT BOXES
WERE EXCHANGED
WITH GERMAN
SOLDIERS

1914

WWI AND THE CHRISTMAS DAY TRUCE

GERMAN CELEBRATIONS IN THE TRENCHES

CHRISTMAS 1914
Hopes that the war would be
over in a few months seemed to be
dashed, but then, on Christmas Eve,
something remarkable happened.
The German and British armies
stopped fighting . . .

Rifleman Leslie Walkington
described the moment he saw the
candles from the German Christmas
trees lighting up the night sky.

*'One of them shouted "A Merry
Christmas English, we're not shooting
tonight." . . . [then] they stuck up a
light. Not to be out-done, so did we.
Then up went another. So we shoved
up another. Soon the lines looked like
an illuminated fete.'*

The sound of rifle shots and
exploding shells stopped, and the
two sides serenaded each other
with Christmas songs. The German
'Silent Night' was met with a
British chorus of 'Auld Lang Syne'.

*'On Christmas Eve I went to the
trenches and the Germans were singing
carols to our men and we singing to
them. Then they shouted to us,
"A Merry Christmas, British comrades.
You English are fine singers."'*
RIFLEMAN E. E. MEADLEY,
QUEEN'S WESTMINSTER RIFLES

A GERMAN
POSTCARD
FROM 1914

'A FRIENDLY
CHAT WITH
THE ENEMY'

1915

**25 September
The Battle of Loos**
The British use gas for the first time but the wind blows it back over their own troops.

1916

**1 July–mid November
The Battle of the Somme**
By the end of the first day nearly 60,000 are dead, wounded or missing. The struggle continued for many long and bitter months, resulting in more than a million casualties and no real winner.

1917

6 April
America formally enters the war.

**31 July–10 November
The Battle of Passchendaele**
One of the most costly campaigns of the war. Both sides suffered huge losses for no strategic gain.

1918

11 November
The Armistice is signed and at 11am the fighting ends.

Millions of men from both sides had been killed or wounded including many of those men who celebrated Christmas 1914 together. For those who survived, the truce was a memory that would stay with them forever.

We will remember them
Once the war was over, scarlet corn poppies were one of the few plants to grow on the devastated battlefields of France and Belgium. The vivid red of the delicate flower came to represent the blood of the fallen soldiers. Today the poppy remains a lasting symbol of remembrance for those who died.

Then men from both sides began to emerge slowly from their trenches and met in no-man's-land. The men shook hands and exchanged food and souvenirs. Both sides saw the lull in fighting as a chance to bury the bodies of their comrades. In some parts of the front the men even staged a football game, kicking around empty bully-beef cans and using their helmets as goalposts.

'Timidly they approached each other – unarmed, of course – until finally a German and an Englishman met and shook hands to the sound of a happy burst of cheering. Within seconds hundreds of people were shaking hands, laughing, exchanging drinks of rum and cognac, cigars and cigarettes, chocolate, sausage and so on.'
RIFLEMAN M. L. WALKINTON,
QUEEN'S WESTMINSTER RIFLES

SOME OF THE SOUVENIRS EXCHANGED BY TROOPS: CAMPAIGN BADGES, UNIFORM BUTTONS AND A GERMAN BELT BUCKLE WITH THE INSCRIPTION 'GOTT MITT UNS' ('GOD WITH US')

Rifleman George Eade of the 3rd London Rifles became friendly with a German soldier. As they parted, the German said to him *'Today we have peace. Tomorrow, you fight for your country, I fight for mine. Good luck.'*

The end of the truce
Sadly, the story did not end there. In some parts of the front the truce lasted a few hours, in others it carried on until the New Year. But everywhere, sooner or later, the fighting resumed.

THE GREATER GAME
FOOTBALL IN THE FIRST WORLD WAR

'There was a time for all things in the world. There was a time for games, there was a time for business, and there was a time for domestic life . . . but there is only time for one thing now, and that thing is war. If the cricketer had a straight eye let him look along the barrel of a rifle. If a footballer had strength of limb let them serve and march in the field of battle.'
SIR ARTHUR CONAN DOYLE

As strange as it may seem today, football played an important part in the First World War. It was used to help recruit volunteers and to drive men on as they went 'over the top' into no-man's-land; and it famously brought together the warring armies during the historic Christmas Day truce of 1914.

The Football Battalion
At the start of the war the football league continued to play but the pressure was soon on for it to be abandoned so that the players and their fans could 'play the greater game'. Footballers began to enlist en masse in Pals Battalions and in December 1914, the 17th Battalion of the Middlesex Regiment, known as 'The Footballers' Battalion' was formed.

One of the first to join was the England centre half Frank Buckley and Clapton Orient (now Leyton Orient FC) were the first English Football League club to enlist together. Many other recruits were club supporters wanting to fight alongside their sporting heroes.

The Fate of the Battalion
On 15 January 1916 the Football Battalion went to the front line. The battalion fought bravely but at great cost. By the end of the war they had lost more than a thousand men, including 462 in one battle alone at the Battle of Arras, 1917.

MEMBERS OF THE 17TH
BATTALION IN PLAYING KIT

RECRUITMENT POSTERS DELIBERATELY
TARGETED FOOTBALL FANS BY COMPARING
WAR TO FOOTBALL

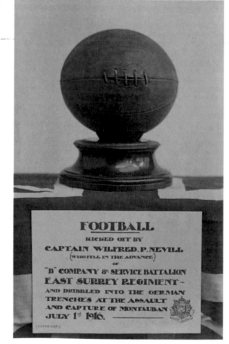

ONE OF THE FOOTBALLS USED DURING THE
FAMOUS 'FOOTBALL' CHARGE TOWARDS THE
GERMAN TRENCHES

The Final Whistle

On Christmas Day 1914 football had brought men from both sides together in friendship. Throughout the war football was a popular form of recreation for troops on both sides. Later it would be used to spur those same men on to play a more deadly game.

ALLIED TROOPS PLAYING FOOTBALL

On 1 July 1916, the first day of the Somme, Captain Wilfred 'Billie' Nevill encouraged his men to go over the top by kicking two footballs into no-man's-land as they began their charge. Their goal was the German line. Nevill was killed within a few steps of leaving the trenches. It was the final game he and many of his men would play.

THIS BRITISH ARMY WHISTLE WAS ISSUED IN 1916, THE YEAR OF THE SOMME. THE WHISTLE WAS BLOWN – JUST LIKE AT THE START OF A FOOTBALL MATCH – TO SIGNAL THE START OF WHAT WOULD BE ONE OF THE BLOODIEST BATTLES OF THE WAR.

FAMOUS FOOTBALLING SOLDIERS

Walter Tull

One of the most celebrated and popular members of the Football Battalion was the ex-Spurs player, Walter Tull. He was one of Britain's first black professional footballers and became the first ever black infantry officer in the British Army. His leadership and courage won him a recommendation for the Military Cross but he never received his medal. He was killed at the Somme in 1918 soon after entering no-man's-land. His body was never found.

Pom Pom Whiting

The goalkeeping star Robert 'Pom Pom' Whiting was another hero of the Football Battalion. He was one of 34,795 killed and missing in action who are commemorated on the Arras Memorial in France.

Vivian Woodward, the England centre forward and Chelsea icon, helped to persuade many a Blues supporter to head for the front by parading around Stamford Bridge perimeter fence with a marching band and calling for new recruits to join up. He survived the war and went on to coach the British Army football team in the Second World War.

Frank Edwards, also known as 'The Footballer of Loos', was a rifleman with London Irish Rifles during the Battle of Loos. He led his battalion across no-man's-land by first kicking a football ahead of the troops.